Harry Potter Spell Book

for Wizarding Kids

The Ultimate Spell book of Curses, Charms, Hexes, and Jinxes for Wizards Training

Amelia

This book Written for Harry Potter fans to know all the Spell name and pronunciation. Added lot of information about spells. This book made for worldwide fans so we did not concentrate grammar on extra note but easy to read.

Copyrights © 2019 Amelia

Content

Introduction

Everybody who's read Harry Potter will have fond memories of rehearsing their wand twirling action in front of the mirror, muttering "Expelliarmus" over and over again in the vague but undying hope that something will actually happen and that magic is indeed real.

Spells in Harry Potter happen in the fictional wizarding world of the series of books by author JK Rowling. Magic spells are used by many of the characters to achieve valuable effects without the help of science and technology. The focal depiction of a "spell" in the Harry Potter books is made up of a gesture made with the character's wand, incorporated with a spoken or mental incantation. In the books and the related film series, the names of the majority of these spells or the incantations used to effect them are gotten from the classical languages, particularly Latin. These phrases are not grammatically correct in any language; many of them use words resembling Latin ones of appropriate meaning but are not proper Latin themselves.

What is a spell?

A spell is a magical action usually accompanied by an incantation (words to say).

Most spells require:

- Concentration
- Wand Movement
- Incantation
- Intention

What is the charm?

A charm is a spell that adds specific properties to its target object, creature, or person. (Change the object and human's behavior.)

What is the transfiguration?

A transfiguration spell modifies the shape or appearance of its targeted objects or person. (It turns something into something else.)

What is a jinx?

A jinx is one kind of black (dark) magic that creates a negative effect.

They are typically amusing to the caster causing a minor inconvenience to the target. It can also be used in defense.

What is a curse?

A curse is a very dangerous Spell, also called as the worst dark magic. It is designed to affect the target in a strongly negative manner.

The Most Recognizable Spells and Charms

This section uses some of the most used, most famous, and most popular spells used in the Harry Potter franchise:

Accio

> Type: Charm
>
> Intonation: AK-ee-oh or AK-see-oh ['akkio]

A summoning spell, which can be used to summon any object towards the caster. Objects in direct line of sight of the caster, as well as things out of view, can be summoned by calling the object aloud after the spell is pronounced.

Mention: Harry Potter called his broom to finish the first task of the Triwizard tournament in 1994 and summon the Portkey to escape Voldemort and the Death Eaters on the Little Hangleton Graveyard in 1995. This spell means "I call" / "I summon" in Latin words.

Alohomora

> Type: Charm
>
> Intonation: ah-LOH-huh-MOR-ah [ə'lo.hə͵moˌɹə]

It is a spell used to open any lock, also called as unlocking charm.

Used by Hermione Granger in 1991 to access to the third-floor corridor at her school, which was banned at the time; she used it again two years later to free Sirius' cell in her teacher's prison room.

Etymology: The spell is derived from the West African Sidiki dialect used in geomancy; it means "kind to thieves," as the author stated during a lawsuit.

Expecto Patronum:

> Type: Charm
>
> Intonation: ex-PEK-toh pa-TROH-num

A spell which is used to cast Patronus; a physical manifestation of one's most positive feelings, which guards the user against Dementors and can be used for communications. The Patronus takes the form of an animal and is unique to each person who casts it.

Seen: Given to Harry by professor Lupine; Harry later taught the army of Dumbledore this charm. This is the only known effective spell against Dementors or Lethifolds.

Etymology: Expecto Patronum means "I await a protector" in Latin.

EXPELLIARMUS

Type: Charm

Intonation: ex-pel-ee-AR-mus [ɛks.ˌpɛ.li.'aˑ.mɪs]

It is a disarming charm which forces whatever the targeted person is holding to fly out of their hands. It is also considered to be Harry Potter's signature spell.

Seen: Used a lot of times from the **Chamber of Secrets** onwards.

Etymology: *expello* means "to expel, to thrust away" and *arma* means "weapons of war" in Latin.

HORCRUX CURSE

Enchantment is never specified, but it is known that the Horcrux Curse divides the user's soul and allows them to trap a piece in an object. This allows them to live even if their mortal body is destroyed, effectively making them immortal unless the Horcruxes are destroyed. Voldemort's immortality is due to his use of the Horcrux Curse to make seven Horcruxes.

LUMOS:

Type: Charm

Intonation: LOO-mos ['lu.məʊs]

It is a wand lightning spell which illuminates the tip of the caster's wand allowing him or her to see in the dark, it's more of like a torch.

Seen: It was first seen in a Chamber of Secrets and then constantly throughout the series.

Etymology: *Light* is called as *lumen* in Latin.

PETRIFICUS TOTALUS:

Type: Curse

Intonation: pe-TRI-fi-cus to-TAH-lus

It is a spell used to temporarily blind and put the victim's body in a certain position which is much like a soldier at attention followed by the victim to fall to the ground after the end of the duration of the spell. This spell was used on Harry Potter by Albus Dumbledore during the first battle of Hogwarts after Draco Malfoy disarmed Harry.

Seen: Used for the first time in 1991 by Hermione, who was trying to prevent Neville from stopping him, Ron and Harry leaving the common room in search of the Philosopher's Stone.

Etymology: English petrify meaning "turn to stone" and full English meaning complete.

PROTEGO:

Type: Charm

Intonation: pro-TAY-goh (IPA: [pɹəʊ.'teɪ.gəʊ])

It is a shielding spell used to create an invisible shield that blocks all physical entities and reflects spells targeted towards the person.

First seen in 1995, in which Harry learned this spell from Hermione in preparation for the third task in the Triwizard Tournament.

Etymology: Protego means "to protect" in Latin.

STUPEFY:

Type: Charm

Intonation: ST(Y)OO-puh-fye

It is a spell that is used to stun the targeted person making them unconscious. This spell can be countered by the counter spell "Rennervate" and it gradually wears off after a short time. The use of this spell can cause severe injury as the force of this spell is additive and exponential.

In 1996, some groups of wizards and witches against Minerva McGonagall (Including Dolores Umbridge). It's also taught by Harry Potter in his D.A. session.

Etymology: Stupefacio means "to make senseless" in Latin.

WINGARDIUM LEVIOSA:

Type: Charm

Intonation: win-GAR-dee-um lev-ee-OH-sa

It is a levitation spell that is used to make an object or person levitate, or fly.

Seen: This spell is given in the opening year charms lessons; this came in handy later that year when Ron Weasley carried out the spell to eliminate a mountain troll; six years later, Harry uses the charm to float the side car of his godfather's flying engine; Ron used it again this year to poke a twig in a tree.

Etymology: Wing means "fly" in English, arduus means "high" in Latin, and levis means "light" in Latin.

The Unforgivable Curses

The Unforgivable Curses are a trifecta of spells that are forbidden in the wizarding world because of their dangerous, horrible nature. They are as listed in follows:

CRUCIO — THE CRUCIATUS CURSE

Type: Curse

Intonation: KROO-see-oh/KROO-shee-OH [/ˈkɹu.si.əʊ/]

A spell which inflicts extreme and intense pain and torture on the recipient of the curse, it doesn't cause physical harm to the victim, but in extreme cases, may drive them insane. The pain is described as having multiple hot burning knives being stabbed into the victim. The spell cannot be cast by someone who's casting it out of anger or spite. Only a person with the true desire to cause the victim pain can cast this spell. Whoever casts this spell will receive a life imprisonment in the Azkaban Prison as it is one of the three unforgiving curses.

Seen: Used lots of times from the 4th book onward.

Etymology: "I torture" called Crucio in Latin originating from crux (genitive crucis), which means "torture platform or stake" or, more specifically "cross".

IMPERIO – THE IMPERIUS CURSE

> **Type:** Curse
>
> **Intonation:** im-PEER-ee-oh [ɪm.'pi.ɹi.ˌəʊ]

One of the three "unforgivable curses" which may lead up to capital punishment or life imprisonment in Azkaban if used on another human, this spell is used to place a victim under the caster's control completely. The spell puts the victim into a trance-like state which he or she cannot come out of by themselves and they become very suggestible to the commands or orders of the caster. Only wizards who are strong-willed may learn to resist this spell.

Seen: Used many times. First seen in 1994 when Barty Crouch Jr, personifying former Auror Alastor Moody, used it on a spider and then on students during a "class demonstration" in a Defense Against the Dark Arts class. When he broke into Gringotts in 1998, Harry used it on a goblin and a Death Eater when they began to suspect.

Etymology: Imperare is Latin word "to order, command and it is the root of few modern words in English. Imperium means command" or "domain,", and imperio means (among other things) "with authority".

Type: Curse

Intonation: ah-VAH-dah kuh-DAHV-rah

The killing curse; causes instant death to the person the spell is cast to accompanied by a green flash of light along with a rushing noise. It is one of the three "Unforgivable Curses" banned by the ministry of curses. There is no known counter curse that can protect the victim from dying, except for a loving sacrifice. Harry porter is the only known survivor of this curse; he was saved from this spell twice, both by his mother's sacrifice, because she was an accidental Horcrux and because his enemy's wand and his wand were made of the same core.

Seen: First said (not by name) in 1991, during the flashback while Hagrid described the death of his parents to Harry; then, the first part of the spell was told by Lucius Malfoy when he tried to kill Harry and several times in each subsequent book.

Etymology: During an interview with the public at the Edinburgh Book Festival on April 15, 2004, JK Rowling said: "Does anyone know where Avada Kedavra came from? It is an ancient spell in Aramaic, and it is the original Abracadabra, which means "Let the thing be destroyed." Originally, it was used to cure diseases and the "thing" was illness, but I decided to do the "thing" as in the person in front of me. I take a lot of freedom with things like those. I turn them and make them mine. "

Lord Voldemort Tried to Kill Harry Potter Using **'Avada Kedavra'** But Failed, Turning Harry Into A Living Legend.

Dueling Spells

These spells are designed to be used in duels and magic fights. Some are offensive in nature, while others are defensive.

CONFRINGO:

Type: Curse

Intonation: con-FRIN-goh

This spell produces a fiery explosion using a tremendous amount of heat.

Seen: Used by Harry Potter to destroy the sidecar of a motorcycle on which he was traveling during a battle against some Death Eaters in 1997; It was later used by Hermione Granger in an attempt to kill Nagini and facilitate an escape from Godric's Hollow.

Etymology: The Latin word "confringo" means, "to break in pieces, to bring to naught".

CONFUNDO:

Type: Charm

Intonation: con-FUN-doh /kʌn.ˈfʌn.dəʊ/

It causes confusion and disorientation. In the Order of the Phoenix, Hermione uses this spell on the aspiring Quidditch Cormac McLaggen to make sure Ron defeats him in the Quidditch tests.

Seen: In 1994, Severus Snape claimed that Harry, Ron, and Hermione had this spell on them to believe in Sirius Black's claim of innocence; used two years later by Hermione to allow Ron to join the Gryffindor Quidditch team. It was used several times in 1997 and 1998.

Etymology: The Latin word "confundo" means, "to confuse, throw into disorder".

DENSAUGEO:

Type: Hex

Intonation: den-SAW-jee-oh /dɛn.ˈsɔ.dʒi.əʊ/

This spell can be used to restore lost teeth or can cause the victim's teeth to grow rapidly.

Seen: Introduced in 1994, when Draco Malfoy's spell recovered over Hermione Granger; Her teeth ran down her neck before she was forced to run to the hospital to shrink. Later used in 1997 to repair the broken teeth of Harry Potter.

Etymology: Latin "dens" means, "tooth" and augeo means to "enlarge".

DEPULSO:

> **Type:** Charm
>
> **Intonation:** deh-PUL-soh

A counter-charm to the summoning spell, it is used to send the target away from the caster.

Seen: Although it is learned in the fourth-year charm class at Hogwarts, it is used several times in 1993, as well as in 1995.

Etymology: From the Latin depulsio, it means "drive away".

DIFFINDO:

> **Type:** Charm
>
> **Intonation:** dif-FIN-doh /dɪ.ˈfɪn.dəʊ/

It is a severing charm, a spell that causes the targeted object to rip or tear.

Seen: Used twice in 1994, the first time Harry Potter cut Cedric Diggory's bag to speak with the latter, and the second time it was Ron Weasley to cut the lace of his tunic's cuffs in an attempt to make them. It seems less feminine. The spell was used a third time by Harry to swap the covers of his new and second-hand copies of Advanced Potion-Making.

Etymology: In Latin diffindo, "I divide:

DURO:

Type: Charm

Intonation: DYOO-roh

It is a hardening charm that turns an object to stone.

Seen: Utilized by Hermione Granger in 1998 while escaping from Death Eaters in the Battle of Hogwarts.

Etymology Latin duro means "I make hard".

EXPULSO:

Type: Curse

Intonation: ecks-PUL-soh (/ɛks.ˈpʊl.səʊ/)

It is an explosion spell that provokes an explosion using a lot of pressure as opposed to heat.

Mentioned: Utilized by Antonin Dolohov during a fight in a cafe in 1997.

Etymology: Latin pulso means "to strike".

FIENDFYRE:

A certain magical spell which unleashes cursed fire that takes shapes of animals and seeks out living targets while burning anything in its path, the fire can also burn indestructible substances such as Horcruxes. It's also very difficult to control and cannot be put out with enchanted or normal water.

FINITE:

Type: Counter-Spell

Intonation: fi-NEE-tay in-can-TAH-tem

It is a counter-spell which terminates all spell effects put out by a caster.

Seen: Severus used this to restore order in his club. Hermione Granger also Utilized this in the film version of Harry and the Chamber of Secrets to destroy Dobby's rogue Bludger after his Quidditch match.

Etymology: Latin finire, means "to finish", and incantatem.

FURNUNCULUS:

Type: Jinx

Intonation: fer-NUN-kyoo-lus

It causes very painful boils to appear on the victim's skin.

Seen: Utilized by Harry on Gregory Goyle.

Etymology: Latin furunculus actual meaning "petty thief" but later used to mean "boil" in English.

IMMOBULUS:

Type: Charm

Intonation: ih-MOH-byoo-luhs

It is a freezing spell that immobilizes and stops the actions of the targeted object or person working on both living and inanimate things.

Seen: Hermione used it in 1992 to freeze 2 Cornish Pixies. Horace Slughorn used icy spells to deactivate a Muggle burglar alarm.

Etymology: From the Latin "immobilis", means immovable.

IMPEDIMENTA:

Type: Jinx

Intonation: im-ped-ih-MEN-tah /ɪm.ˌpɛ.dɪ.'mɛn.ta

A spell used to slow down or stop a target.

Seen: Used in 1995 when Harry was practicing for the Third Task of the Triwizard Tournament. In 1996, Harry potter saw in memory that James Potter used it in Severus Snape. Also Utilized in 1997 by Harry against the Inferi and Snape. The strongest uses of this spell seem capable of flying targets.

Etymology: Latin impedimentum (plural impedimenta) means "a hindrance" or "an impediment".

INCARCEROUS:

Type: Conjuration

Intonation: in-KAR-ser-us

A conjuration spell used to tie up the target with ropes conjured from thin air.

Seen: It was first heard in 1996 when Dolores Umbridge tries to stop the centaurs. Also used by Harry in the Inferi in the Voldemort Crystal Cave in 1997 and also tried using it in Severus Snape in the same year.

Etymology: Maybe English incarcerate, "to imprison".

JELLY-LEGS JINX [LOCOMOTOR WIBBLY]

Type: Curse, Jinx

Intonation: loh-koh-MOH-tor WIB-lee

It causes the victim's legs to wobble like jelly, stopping them from walking.

Seen: One of the spells mentioned in Curses and Against Curses by Vindictus Viridian, used in Harry, practicing for the Third Task of the Triwizard Tournament, by Hermione. In addition, Draco Malfoy was beaten with this curse (along with another) at the end of the period.

LEVICORPUS:

Type: Jinx

Intonation: levi-COR-pus (nonverbal) [lɛvɪ.'kɔɹ.pɪs]

A spell created by Severus Snape, it is used to hoist the targeted person into the air by their ankle.

Seen: Apparently invented by the Half-Blood Prince; it is a non-verbal-only spell (although it is whispered by Hermione in 1997).

Harry learned it by reading the notes written by the Half-Blood Prince. He used it on Ron. The previous year, Harry had seen (through the Pensieve used by Severus Snape) his father, James Potter, to use the spell against Professor Snape. In the Order of the Phoenix movie, Luna Lovegood somehow uses this against a Death Eater, although she speaks it, and the spell's name is unknown to any students until the Half-Blood Prince.

LIBERACORPUS:

> **Type**: Counter-Jinx
>
> **Intonation**: lib-er-ah-COR-pus (nonverbal)

It is the counter-spell to "Levicorpus".

Seen: Harry potter utilized the spell in 1996 to counter Levicorpus who had inadvertently cast on Ron.

Etymology: Latin liberare means "to free", and Latin corpus means "body".

LOCOMOTOR MORTIS:

> **Type**: Curse
>
> **Intonation**: loh-koh-MOH-tor MOR-tis

It is a spell used to stick the targeted person's legs together.

Seen: Used by Draco in Neville Longbottom in 1991. Used by Harry Potter in Draco Malfoy, who diverted it, in 1996. One of the spells in Pottermore.

OPPUGNO:

> **Type:** Jinx
>
> **Intonation:** oh-PUG-noh : /ə.ˈpʊg.no/

It is a spell used to make the targeted object to attack a victim.

Etymology: Latin oppugno, means "I attack".

PIERTOTUM LOCOMOTOR:

> **Type:** Charm
>
> **Intonation:** pee-ayr-TOH-tum (or peer-TOH-tum)

It is a powerful spell used to bring inanimate objects to life for aid. During the battle of Hogwarts, this spell was cast to animate the suits of armor and statues within Hogwarts to defend the castle by Professor McGonagall.

Seen: In the Battle of Hogwarts, Professor McGonagall used this spell to animate the armour and statues inside Hogwarts, to defend the castle. Possibly used by Albus Dumbledore to enchant the statues at the fountain at the entrance of the Department of the Ministry of Magic.

Etymology: Pier means "friend" or "colleague", totum refers to "the whole" or "total", and locomotor means "the movement"

PROTEGO HORRIBILIS:

Type: Charm

Intonation: pro-TAY-goh horr-uh-BIL-lis 'teɪ.gəʊ ˌhɔɹ.ə.ˈbɪ.lɪs]

It is one of the most powerful shield charms which can be used against dark magic.

Seen: Issued by Professor Flitwick in an attempt to strengthen the castle's defenses at the Battle of Hogwarts.

Etymology: Protego means "I protect", and Horribilis, "horrible , frightful, dreadful" in Latin.

PROTEGO MAXIMA:

Intonation: pro-TAY-goh MAX-ee-Ma

Type: Charm

Another powerful shielding spell that can be used against dark magic. It is a bigger and stronger version of Protego; when combined with other wizards casting it at the same time; it can become so powerful that anyone who comes in contact with the shield or tries to enter it would be disintegrated. It was used by Professor McGonagall, Professor Slughorn, Mrs. Weasley, and Professor Flitwick all together to strengthen the castle's defenses during the Battle of Hogwarts.

Seen: Issued by Professor Flitwick, Professor McGonagall, Professor Slughorn, and Mrs. Weasley in an attempt to strengthen the castle's defenses at the Battle of Hogwarts.

Etymology: Protego means"I protect In Latin "

Protego Totalum:

Type: Charm

Intonation: pro-TAY-goh toh-TAH-lum

It is another powerful shielding spell that protects an area for an extended period of time.

Seen: In 1997, this was one of the spells used by Hermione Granger and Harry Potter to protect their camp from unwanted visitors.

Etymology: Protego means "to protect" and Latin totus means "as a whole" In Latin.

Reducto:

Type: Curse

Intonation: re-DUK-toh [ɹɛ.'dʌk.təʊ]

It is a spell that breaks and disintegrates inanimate objects.

Seen: In 1995, Harry used it in one of the hedges of the Three Wizards labyrinth and ends up burning a small hole; In 1995, Gryffindors in the year of Harry Potter referred to Parvati Patil as able to reduce a table full of dark detectors to ashes, and Harry and his friends used the spell in the Department of Mysteries against Death Eaters, shattering many Orbs of Prophecy in the process; In 1997, a member of the Order of the Phoenix tried to use this spell to knock down a door that the Death Eaters had blocked when the Death Eaters cornered Dumbledore in the Tower of the Striped Lightning.

Etymology: Reductio means "to restore" in Latin.

RICTUSEMPRA:

> **Type:** Charm
>
> **Intonation:** ric-tuhs-SEM-pra

It is a spell used to make the target feel ticklish until they become weak with laughter.

Seen: By Harry Potter in Draco Malfoy in 1992, when they fought in the Duel Club.

Etymology: Latin rictus means "open mouth", and Latin semper means "always".

RIDIKKULUS:

It is a spell used specifically when fighting Boggart, the spell forces the Boggart to take the appearance of an object or thing the caster of the spell is focusing on. Results can only be achieved if the caster is imagining or focusing on something which is humorous with the intention or desire that would weaken the Boggart.

Salvio Hexia:

Type: Charm

Intonation: SAL-vee-oh HECKS-ee-ah

It is a spell used to protect oneself from hexes.

Seen: Harry and Hermione cast this spell to strengthen their camp's defenses against intruders in 1997.

Etymology: Latin salvus meaning "safe" and English hex meaning "a magic spell".

Sectumsempra:

Type: Curse

Intonation: sec-tum-SEMP-rah [ˌsɛktəmˈsɛmpɹa]

It is a spell that lacerates the targeted person; the cut is so intense that it feels like the victim has been slashed by a sword. The victim might bleed to death cause of the wound. Severus Snape invented this curse and used it against his personal enemies. The movement of the wand affects how the victim is cut.

Seen/Mentioned: Used by Harry in 1997 against Draco Malfoy, and then against the Inferi in Lord Voldemort's Horcrux chamber, and Snape used it against George Weasley (it was not intentional; he pointed to a Death Eater who tried to curse Lupine) on the Order's flight from Privet Drive. Harry learned it in the old Snape Potions textbook. In 1998, it is said that the spell is the "characteristic" spell of Severus Snape.

Etymology: Latin sectum, "cut", and semper, "always".

Serpensortia:

Type: Conjuration

Intonation: ser-pen-SOR-shah [ˌsɛɹpənˈsɒɹtʃa]

It is a conjuring spell that conjures a serpent from the caster's wand. Draco conjured the serpent called Serpensortia using this spell during a duel with Harry Potter.

Seen: Used by Draco Malfoy during a duel with Harry in 1992.

Etymology: Latin serpens meaning "a snake" and Latin ortis meaning "source".

Slugulus Eructo:

Type: Curse

It is a slug-vomiting charm that forces the victim to burp up slimy waste.

Seen: In 1992, Ronald Weasley tried to curse Draco Malfoy with this spell after he insulted Hermione Granger but was unsuccessful since his wand broke at that time and, therefore, his curse failed against himself.

Stinging Jinx:

Type: Jinx

Makes the victim swell to the point that it is unrecognizable. In the Deathly Hallows, Hermione Granger uses this jinx on Harry to hide his identity from the Death Eaters.

Seen: Harry Potter inadvertently used one in Severus Snape throughout the Oclumance lessons in 1996. It was not debilitating because instance but is stronger when it was purposefully cast, as evidenced by the results of the Hermione Granger stinging spell made use of in Harry Potter in 1998 to Misshaping on purpose Harry's appearance. Lucius Malfoy calls him Painful Jinx in Harry Potter and also the Deathly Hallows.

Tarantallegra:

    Type: Jinx

    Intonation: ta-RON-ta-LEG-gra

It is a dancing feet spell which makes the targeted person's legs twitch wildly out of that person's control; it would seem like they are dancing.

Seen: First used by Draco Malfoy in Harry Potter at the Duel Club in 1992.

Etymology: English "tarantella" significance "a quick swirling dancing" and Italian Allegra definition "joyful".

Waddiwasi:

    Type: Jinx

    Intonation: wah-deh-WAH-see

It is a spell used to shoot soft, small masses of whatever the caster of the spell desires at the targeted person.

Seen/Mentioned: Issued by Remus Lupine in 1993, about Peeves the Poltergeist, sending a bundle of chewing gum through his nose.

Etymology: English wad meaning "a lump of soft material" and Latin vado meaning, "to go".

When Fighting Dragons, Duelling Spells Certainly Come in Handy

Miscellaneous Spells

This is a list of spells that don't quite fit into any other category, but are fantastic all the same:

AGUAMENTI:

Type: Charm, Conjuration

Intonation: AH-gwah-MEN-tee   /a.gwə.'mɛn.ti/

Conjures a stream of water from the wizard's wand.

Etymology: The Latin word aqua, which has been transformed into modern languages such as Portuguese as water, which means "water", combined with a form of the Latin verb mentio which means "to speak, mention or proclaim."

ANAPNEO:

Type: Healing Spell, Vanishment

Intonation: ah-NAP-nee-oh (IPA: /ə.'næp.ni.əʊ/)

Un-chokes a person, enabling them to breathe again by removing whatever's obstructing their airway.

Seen/Mentioned: Used by Horace Slughorn, released on Marcus Belby when the latter choked on a pheasant in 1996.

Etymology: From the Greek verb anapneo, meaning "I breathe in."

ARRESTO MOMENTUM:

Type: Charm

Intonation: ah-REST-oh mo-MEN-tum

It is a slowing charm which decreases the velocity of a moving target. It can be used on multiple targets, as well as on the caster themselves.

Seen: Used by Dumbledore to save one of his students from a fall in 1993; Hermione Granger used it, with little effect, in 1998 to cushion a deadly fall.

Etymology: Probably the combination of the Anglo-French arester, which means "stop" and the Latin impetus, which means "the force or force gained while moving"; The literal translation is therefore "Bring the force or force obtained while stopping."

Ascendio:

Type: Charm

Intonation: ah-SEN-dee-oh

It is used to moves a target upwards.

Seen: Utizied by Harry in the 2nd Task of the Triwizard Tournament to propel him to the surface of the lake in 1995.

Etymology: Derived from Latin ascendo, meaning "to climb"

Avis:

Type: Conjuration

Intonation: AH-viss /a'vɪs/

A flock of little birds conjures up.

Seen: Utilized in 1994 by Mr. Ollivander to test Viktor Krum's wand. Also offensively employed by Hermione against Ron Weasley.

Etymology: The Latin word avis means "bird".

Bombarda:

Type: Charm

Intonation: bom-BAR-dah

Causes a very worst explosion.

Seen: Utilized by Hermione to free Sirius Black from prison in 1994. This spell was only seen in the film.

BUBBLE—HEAD CHARM:

Type: Charm

Creates an air bubble around the user's head, allowing him to breathe underwater.

It was utilized by Cedric and Fleur during the second Triwizard challenge to allow them to swim at the bottom of the Great Lake.

CATERWAULING CHARM:

Type: Charm

Lay a magic curfew on a limited area; if someone breaks the charm by coming out of their house, appearing or twisting, it causes a loud whimper.

In the Deathly Hallows, Harry, Ron and Hermione activate a Caterwauling spell when they appear in Hogsmeade.

COLLORPORTUS:

Utilized to lock doors. In the *Order of the Phoenix* Hermione uses the charm in a tried to lock out the Death Eaters that chase them through the Ministry.

CUSHIONING CHARM:

Cushions a fall.

DELETRIUS:

Type: Charm

Intonation: deh-LEE-tree-us

It is a counter-charm to the Reverse spell. It vanishes the image of the spell which was casted prior to it and may also perish other certain images.

Seen: This spell was only seen in 1994 when Amos Diggory used Prior Incantato to detect that Winky had thrown Morsmordre using Harry Potter's wand.

Etymology: Latin delere, meaning "to destroy", and English "detritus", meaning rubble.

DEPRIMO:

Type: Charm

Intonation: deh-PREEM-oh

This spell is used to blast holes in the ground.

Seen: Hermione Granger opened a hole through the floor of the living room of Xenophilius Lovegood's house in 1998 using this spell.

Etymology: The incantation, when non-capitalized, means "to depress" or "depress".

DESCENDO:

Type: Charm

Intonation: deh-SEN-doh

A spell that causes the targeted object to move downwards.

Seen: In 1997, Ron used it to magically descend the stairs of his room, which lead to his family's attic; later that year, Crabbe used it in an attempt to cause a wall of trash behind which Ron was hiding to fall on him.

Etymology: Descendo is Latin for "I descend".

DISILLUSIONMENT CHARM:

Type: Charm

The disillusion charm makes the user invisible by camouflaging them perfectly in their environment. In Order of the Phoenix, Moody casts this charm on Harry to make him invisible.

Seen: Used and mentioned several times from 1995 onwards.

DISSENDIUM:

Type: Charm

Intonation: dih-SEN-dee-um

The effect of this spell is to open secret passageways or to open things in general.

Seen: Utilized several times in 1993 to open up the Gunhilda statue of Gorsemoor, then again four years later on in an unsuccessful attempt to open up the Salazar Slytherin necklace.

Etymology: There are numerous suggestions.

ENGORGIO:

> **Type:** Charm
>
> **Intonation:** en-GOR-jee-oh

Makes an object or person to grow larger.

Seen: Rubeus Hagrid used this spell on his pumpkins in 1992; Two years later, Barty Crouch Jr cast this spell on a spider for students to see more easily when he cast a curse on him. Used in another spider three years later to test a new wand.

Etymology: English word engorge meaning "to fill to excess".

EPISKEY:

> **Type:** Healing Spell
>
> **Intonation:** ee-PIS-key

A spell used to heal minor injuries.

Seen: In 1996, Nymphadora Tonks used this spell to fix Harry's broken nose after Draco Malfoy broke it at the Hogwarts Express, Harry, in turn, used it to heal Demelza Robins swollen lip after Ron hit her during Quidditch practice.

Etymology: The word derived from Greek "episkeui" ("επισκευή"), which means "repair".

ERECTO:

Type: Charm

Intonation: eh-RECK-toh

This spell is used to erect upright structures or mostly tents.

Seen: Used by Hermione to build a shelter for her, Harry and Ronald Weasley in 1997.

Etymology: Latin erectus meaning "to set up, to raise".

EVANESCO:

Type: Transfiguration

Intonation: ev-an-ES-koh

A spell which is used to vanish objects or making them invisible.

Seen: Used by William Weasley to fade a pack of old scrolls while cleaning 12 Grimmauld Place in 1995.

Etymology: Latin evanesco meaning "to vanish".

FERULA:

Type: Conjuration, Healing spell

Intonation: fer-ROOL-lah

It is a bandaging charm that conjures and wraps bandages around a wound while splinting any broken or fractured bones.

Seen: Used by Remus Lupine in 1994 to tie the broken leg of Ronald Weasley.

Etymology: Latin ferula means "walking-stick" or "splint".

FIDELIUS CHARM:

> **Type:** Charm

It is a very complicated spell that is used to hide secret information or knowledge within the soul of the charm's recipient. Unless the Secret-Keeper/the recipient willingly chooses to reveal the secret, the information would be irretrievable. When Harry Potter was an infant, his parents and he were hidden from Voldemort with this spell. Even if the secret keeper dies, the secret key that he or she holds can never be revealed to anyone else and upon the keeper's death all those who have been told the secret become keepers in turn.

Seen: In 1993, it was explained that when Harry was simply a baby, he and his parents were hidden from Voldemort with this charm; From 1995 onwards, it was used to protect Grimmauld Place, and in 1998 it was used to protect Shell Cottage.

Etymology: Latin fidelis, which means "faithful".

FLAGRATE:

> **Type:** Charm
>
> **Intonation:** flah-GRAH-tay

A spell which uses the wand to write in midair with firey marks.

Seen: Tom Riddle utilized this spell to write his name; Hermione used it three years later to mark some doors.

Etymology: From the Latin flagrate, meaning "a burn".

FLYING CHARM:

Type: Charm

The Flying Charm is what permits broomsticks to levitate.

Seen: Draco mentions this spell when he insults Ron Weasley's broomstick, wondering why anyone would love it.

GEMINIO:

Type: Charm

Intonation: jeh-MIH-nee-oh

A doubling charm/spell which duplicates the targeted object, it is used to duplicate objects indefinitely. It is also known as the Gemino Curse. Hermione Granger once used it on Salazar Slytherin's locket to disguise her presence from Dolores Umbridge.

Etymology: The Latin word gemini means "twins".

GLISSEO:

Type: Charm

A spell which is used to flatten the steps on a stairway turning it into a slide.

Seen: Utilized by Hermione Granger to escape the Death Eaters.

Etymology: Probably derived from French glisser, meaning "to slide".

HOMENUM REVELIO:

> **Type:** Charm

> **Intonation:** HOM-eh-num reh-VEH-lee-oh

A human- presence-revealing spell which reveals the presence of any human in the vicinity of the caster.

HOT AIR CHARM:

> **Type:** Charm

Shoot a jet of hot air from the caster's wand.

Seen: Used by Hermione Granger in 1995 to dry her tunic. It is also utilized shortly after to melt the snow. It was also utilized by Albus Dumbledore in 1997 to dry Harry's robe and his own robe. Very possibly a form of Ventus.

HOVER CHARM:

> **Type:** Charm

Causes an object to float. In the Chamber of Secrets, Harry is almost driven from Hogwarts when it is mistakenly thought that he has cast this charm in the presence of his aunt and uncle.

Seen/Mentioned: Used by Dobby to demolish a pudding.

HURLING HEX:

Type: Hex

Swings a kite out of their broom. In the Philosopher's Stone Professor Quirrell is likely to cast this spell to get Harry out of his broom during his first Quidditch ball game.

Seen: Professor Flitwick suggested that Harry's confiscated Firebolt might be angry at this spell.

Notes: May be related to the broom jinx.

IMPERVIUS:

Type: Charm

Intonation: im-PUR-vee-u

It is a spell used to make an object repel mist or water. Used by Hermione Granger once on Harry's glasses while he was in a Quidditch match and also by the Gryffindor Quidditch team.

Seen: Utilized by Hermione in 1993 in Harry's glasses during a Quidditch match and also by the Gryffindor Quidditch team. Also used in 1997, first by Ron to protect Yaxley's office objects from the rain, and then by Hermione to protect Harry potter, Ron and Griphook from the burning treasure in the Lestranges vault.

Etymology: It is said that the Latin impervius means (and is the source of) "impervious"; although it is the source of the word, it is better translated as impassable, as in a mountain peak.

INCENDIO:

Type: Charm, Conjuration

Intonation: in-SEN-dee-oh

It is a spell used to produce fire out of the wand. Bellatrix once used the non-verbal version of this spell on Hagrid's hut.

Seen/Mentioned: It was first seen in 1994 by Arthur Weasley to create a fire in the Dursleys' home so he could use Floo's dust there. In 1997, this spell was used several times in battle, especially when Hagrid's cabin caught fire. Possibly it was also used by Hagrid in 1991 to create a home fire before taking Harry to London.

INTRUDER CHARM:

Type: Charm

Alerts the user when an intruder has entered a home or a particular location.

Seen: Horace Slughorn used it in a house owned by Muggles where he stayed temporarily in 1996, but did not hear it shot when Albus Dumbledore and Harry Potter arrived, as he was in the bathroom.

LANGLOCK:

Type: Jinx

Intonation: LANG-lock

A spell that sticks the targeted person's tongue to the roof of their mouth. This spell was exclusively created by Severus Snape.

Seen: Utilized by Harry in Peeves and twice in Argus Filch, for general applause.

Etymology: Probably from the French langue ("tongue") and the English "lock".

LEGILIMENS:

Type: Charm

Intonation: Le-JIL-ih-mens

It is a spell that allows the caster to get inside the mind of the targeted person, along him or her to see the thoughts, memories, and emotions of the victim.

Seen: Used by Severus Snape about Harry after he had a dream about Arthur Weasley's attack by Nagini in 1995. Also, during the Oclumance lessons in 1996. Also used nonverbally by Snape about Harry in 1997 to allow him to see where Harry had learned the Sectumsempra spell.

Etymology: Latin legere ("to read") and mens ("mind").

LOCOMOTOR:

Type: Charm

Intonation: loh-kuh-MOH-tor

Similar to the Summoning spell, this spell allows the caster to levitate a target a few inches off the ground and then move the object in any desired direction, the object has to be called aloud after the incantation of the spell for it to work.

Seen: Used by Nymphadora Tonks in Harry Potter to move Harry potter's trunk from his room. Filius Flitwick used it in a similar way to move Sybill Trelawney's trunk after Dolores Umbridge fired her. Parvati Patil and Lavender Brown used this spell to run their cases around the edges of the table. A variation seen in 1998 is Locomotor Piertotum, which caused the animation of the Hogwarts statues.

Etymology: Latin locus (place) and moto, "set in motion" (passive motor), or English locomotion.

LUMOS MAXIMA:

Type: Charm

Intonation: LOO-mos Ma-cks-ima

This spell is a more powerful version of Lumos and Lumos duo; it produces a blinding and powerful white light from the tip of the caster's wand.

Seen: First practiced by Harry in the Dursleys' house, then used by Dumbledore to illuminate the Horcrux cave.

Etymology: Lumos + maxima, Latin "greatest."

METEOLOJINX RECANTO:

Type: Counter-Charm

Intonation: mee-tee-OH-loh-jinks reh-CAN-toh.

Reverses weather-related spells. In the Deathly Hallows, Hermione recommends that Ron try this spell to prevent a ministerial office from raining.

Seen: Suggested in 1997 by Arthur Weasley to Ron (disguised as Reginald Cattermole through the use of multiplayer potion) as the best way to clear up the bad rain in an office of the Ministry. Also used by Bartemius Crouch Jr (disguised as Alastor Moody) in 1994 to cease the effect of the Great Hall's roof climate insisting that it is broken when he told Dumbledore to "fix his roof."

Etymology: Meteorology, the study of weather, the word jinx and recant, "to withdraw or retract". Interestingly in modern English recant means to say that you no longer hold a belief.

MIMBLEWIMBLE:

Type: Curse

Intonation: MIM-bull-wim-bull

It is a magical spell used to tie the victim's tongue in a knot to prevent them from making any coherent.

Seen: Seen in 1997 as a deterrent to Severus Snape, or any other unwanted visitor to 12 Grimmauld Place, for betraying its location to anyone else.

MOBILIARBUS:

Type: Charm

Intonation: mo-bil-lee-AR-bus

It is a spell that is used to levitate wooden objects a few inches off the ground to push them or move them in any given direction.

Seen: In 1993, Hermione used the spell to move a Christmas Tree in The Three Brooms next to her table to hide Harry, who was in Hogsmeade illegally.

Etymology: Latin mobilis, "movable" or "flexible", and arbor (alternatively arbos), "tree".

MOBILICORPUS:

Type: Charm

Intonation: moh-bil-lee-COR-pus

Similar to Mobiliarbus, this spell levitates and moves dead or unconscious bodies.

Seen: Sirius Black used it on Severus Snape in 1994. Lord Voldemort probably used it on Peter Pettigrew in the cemetery to move it forward.

Etymology: Latin mobilis, "movable", and corpus, "body".

MORSMORDE:

Intonation: morz-MOR-druh

Invokes the dark mark; the symbol of Voldemort and his followers.

Seen: Used by Barty Crouch Jr in 1994. Also seen in 1997 over the castle to attract Albus Dumbledore to his death. Apparently, it was invented by Lord Voldemort.

Etymology: Latin mors, "death", and mordere, meaning "to bite" (or its French derivative mordre); this would appear to be associated with the name of Lord Voldemort's followers, the Death Eaters. The English murder might also contribute.

MUFFLIATO:

Type: Charm

Intonation: muf-lee-AH-to

It is a spell used to fill people's ears with an unidentifiable buzzing so as to stop them from hearing nearby conversations.

Seen: It was used in 1996 by Harry Potter and Ron Weasley in various teachers and people like Madam Pomfrey. It was created by Severus Snape. As Hermione noted, it is probably not approved by the Ministry of Magic. It was also used in 1997 by Hermione Granger to protect the camp where she and Harry were hidden.

NOX:

Type: Charm

Intonation: NOCKSS

It is a counter-spell for the wand- lighting spell "Lumos", used to extinguish wand light.

Seen: In 1994, Harry Potter and Hermione Granger used this spell to turn off their wand lights in the House of Screams. Used in 1998 when Harry was in the passage under the Whomping Willow that leads to the House of Screams. The power of Lumos can be organized so that a powerful wizard can make the spell glow brightly or wizards like the volume of enchantment. For example, "LUMOS !!!" It would be powerful and the "lumos" would be weaker. Also used by Harry Potter in 1998 to turn off the light to hide the Marauder Map of Severus Snape.

Etymology: Latin nox, meaning "night".

OBLIVIATE:

Type: Charm

Intonation: oh-BLI-vee-ate

It is a memory spell used to erase specific memories of the targeted person.

Seen: First seen in 1993 when it was used by Gilderoy Lockhart in Harry and Ron; The spell failed due to a defective wand, which cost Lockhart most of his own memory. In addition, Hermione Granger used this spell to erase her parents' memories in 1997. Again, it was used in 1997 when Hermione used the spell on 2 Death Eaters who had followed Harry, Ron, and Hermione after their escape from Bill Weasley's and Fleur Delacour's wedding.

Etymology: Latin oblivisci, "forget". The spell is most often used against Muggles who have seen something of the Wizarding world.

OBSCURO:

Type: Conjuration

Intonation: ob-SKYUR-oh

It is a conjuration spell that is used to blindfold the target. This spell mostly affects characters in paintings.

Seen: Used by Hermione in 1997 to obstruct the portrait of Phineas Nigellus's view of her location.

Notes: This spell can only affect the characters in the paintings; There are no other references to this spell.

ORCHIDEOUS:

Type: Conjuration

Intonation: or-KID-ee-us

It is a conjuring spell that conjures a bouquet of flowers.

Seen: Used in 1994 by Mr. Ollivander to test Fleur Delacour's wand. Probably not verbally used by Tom Riddle to give flowers to Mrs. Smith.

Etymology: English orchid and Latin suffix -eous, "of or bearing (the root word)".

PERICULUM:

Type: Charm

Intonation: pur-ICK-you-lum

A spell that produces a burst of red sparks from the tip of the wand.

Seen: Used during the third task of the Triwizard Tournament by Harry Potter.

Etymology: Periculum is Latin for "danger".

PERMANENT STICKING CHARM:

Type: Charm

Sticks posters, paintings and other items on walls indefinitely. In Harry Potter and the Deathly Hallows, it is revealed that Sirius Black has stuck posters to his bedroom wall with a lasting charm to prevent his mother from taking them down.

Seen: First discussed in 1995, when Sirius Black presumed that his mommy's paint was fixed to the wall surface with such a Charm. It is implied that the picture in the Muggle Head of state's office also has such an appeal on it.

POINT ME:

Type: Spell

Have the user's wand turn in his hand to point north. In the Goblet of Fire, Harry potter uses this spell in the final triwizard challenge to help navigate the maze.

Seen/Mentioned: Hermione Granger taught it to Harry Potter, who used it throughout the Triwizard Tournament, specifically to browse the hedge puzzle during the Third Task.

PORTUS:

> **Type**: Charm
>
> **Intonation**: POR-tus

It is a spell used to turn the targeted object into a portkey.

Seen: Used by Dumbledore in 1996.

Etymology: Latin porta, meaning "gate", or portare, meaning "to carry". There is a Latin word portus, meaning "harbour", but it is inappropriate in this context.

PRIORI INCANTATEM:

> **Type**: Charm
>
> **Intonation**: pri-OR in-can-TAH-toh

Reveal the last spell cast by the wand.

Seen: Hermione Granger showed it to Harry Potter, who used it during the Triwizard Competition, particularly to browse the hedge maze during the Third Job.

Etymology: In Latin prior means "previous", and incantare means "ask a spell"

QUIETUS:

Type: Charm

Intonation: KWIY-uh-tus

It is the counter-spell to the amplifying charm; it makes the targeted person or object sound quieter.

Seen: Used in 1994 by Ludo Bagman.

Etymology: Latin quietus, "calm" or "quiet".

REDUCIO:

Type: Charm

Intonation: re-DOO-see-oh

It is a shrinking charm that makes an object shrink in size, a counter-spell to Engorgement Charm.

Seen: In Harry Potter as well as the Deathly Hallows: Component 1, Harry Potter, after inspecting his Blackthorn stick on the Bluebell flames with Engorgio, casts this spell to reduce the formerly enlarged flames.

Etymology: English reduce, "to shrink". (Latin has a verb reducere, present tense reduco. This is the source of the English "reduce".

RELASHIO:

Type: Jinx

Intonation: ruh-LASH-ee-oh

It is a spell used to force the targeted person to lose the grip on whatever he or she is holding.

Seen: Utilized by Harry Potter against Grindylows in the second task of the Triwizard Competition. Additionally utilized in 1997 as well as 1998, when Hermione utilized this spell to complimentary Mrs. Cattermole from the chained chair as well as to release the Ukrainian Ironbelly on which they were to venture out from Gringotts.

Etymology: Probably from the French verb relâcher ="to release, to set free", or Italian rilascio (pronounced the same way as the spell)= "I release".

Rennervate:

Type: Charm

Intonation: RENN-a-vate

It is a reviving spell used to awaken an unconscious person, a counter charm to the Stunning Spell.

Seen: In 1994, Amos Diggory used it to wake Winky and Dumbledore used it to wake Viktor Krum. Harry then used it to try to wake a damn Dumbledore in the cave by the sea.

Etymology: Officially renamed from Ennervate by J.K. Rowling. Rennervate means "to energize", whilst the former Ennervate, meant "to weaken,".

Reparo:

Type: Charm

Intonation: reh-PAH-roh

It is a mending charm used to seamlessly repair broken objects. Hermione once used this spell to fix Harry's broken wand.

Seen: Countless times throughout the books. Broken objects are often described as "flying" back together. However, the substances contained in the broken objects do not re-enter. In 1995 Harry broke a bowl of murtlap essence. He could repair the bowl, but the essence of murtlap was splattered on the floor.

Etymology: Latin reparo meaning "to renew" or "repair".

REPELLO MUGGLETUM:

> **Type:** Charm
>
> **Intonation:** ruh-PEL-oh MUH-guhl-tuhm

A muggle repelling spell used to keep muggles away from wizards and wizarding places by causing them to remember crucial meetings they had missed and also to cause the muggles in question to totally forget what they were doing.

Seen: Mentioned in Quidditch Through the Ages as used to keep Muggles out of the Quidditch World Cup. It was also said that Hogwarts was guarded by the spell that repels muggles. It was also used by Harry and Hermione on numerous occasions, among many other spells, to protect and hide their camp in 1997.

REVELIO:

> **Type:** Charm
>
> **Intonation:** reh-VEL-ee-oh

A spell which is used to reveal secrets about the targeted person or object.

SCOURGIFY:

Type: Charm

Intonation: SKUR-ji-fy

It is a spell used to clean objects.

Seen: First used by Nymphadora Tonks to clean Hedwig's cage in 1995. Later, Ginny Weasley performed the spell to clean the Stinksap at the Hogwarts Express, also used by James Potter in Severus Snape after yelling at him several curses and obscenities.

Etymology: Perhaps related to English scour, "clean". -ify is a common English suffix meaning "to make ...". Therefore scourgify could mean "to make clean".

SILENCIO:

Type: Charm

Intonation: sih-LEN-see-oh

It is a silencing charm that is used to make something silent. Hermione used this spell once to silent a frog and a raven in Charms class.

Seen: First used by Hermione in 1996 to silence a frog and a crow in the Enchantments class, then used to silence a Death Eater trying to tell his comrades where they were.

Etymology: Probably Latin silentium, "silence". Also, silencio and silêncio mean "silence" in Spanish and Portuguese, respectively.

SONOROUS:

Type: Charm

It is an amplifying spell that makes the targeted person or object sound louder. A counterspell to the Quietening spell, Quietus.

Seen: Harry Potter and the Prisoner of Azkaban (video game)

Notes: Not to be confused with the Amplifying Charm, Sonorus.

TELEPORTATION SPELL:

Type: Spell

Teleports items from one place to another. Although the enchantment is never revealed, Dumbledore uses this spell to transport Harry's trunk and owl to the Burrow.

Seen: In 1996, Albus Dumbledore used this to transport Harry Potter's school supplies, clothes, and owl to the Burrow.

TERGEO:

Type: Charm

Intonation: TUR-jee-oh

It is a spell used to clean objects or draws off liquid.

Seen: Hermione used the spell in 1996 to remove blood from Harry's face. It is later used to remove spilled ink from the parchment. It was also used in 1997 to clean a Ron handkerchief and dust off a photo of Gellert Grindelwald in the house of Bathilda Bagshot of Harry Potter.

Etymology: Latin tergere, "wipe off; cleanse".

TRIP JINX:

Type: Jinx

It is a spell that forces the targeted person to trip and fall.

Seen: Seen in 1996. It was cast successfully on Harry by Draco, when he and other members of the Inquisitorial Squad attempted to round up members of Dumbledore's Army.

UNBREAKABLE VOW:

Type: Charm

Kill the participant or participants if they break a promise. In the Half-Blood Prince, Severus Snape swears an unbreakable vote to help Draco Malfoy kill Dumbledore.

Seen: Towards the end of Harry Potter and the goblet of fire, Hermione casts the spell into a jar, in which she puts Rita Skeeter in her Animagus beetle form to prevent her from becoming human.

Undetectable Extension Charm

It causes an object to expand inside while remaining the same size outside. Arthur Weasley performs this charm in his car to accommodate his entire family in it while driving to Kings Cross station.

Vulnera Sanentur:

Type: Healing Spell

Intonation: VUL-ner-ah sah-NEN-tour

It is a healing spell that knits wounds, slows blood flow, and clears residue. A counter-spell to Sectumsempra. Severus Snape used this spell on Draco Malfoy who was subjected to the spell Sectumsempra cast by Harry Potter during dueling.

Seen: Used by Snape to heal Draco's wounds caused by the Sectumsempra curse launched by Harry Potter in 1997.

Etymology: Vulnera Sanentur derives from the Latin. Vulnus means "wound," and sanare means "to heal"

Other Charms, Curses, Hexes, and Jinxes

ABERTO

Type: Charm

Intonation: Ah-bare-toh

It is a spell used to open doors.

AQUA ERUCTO

Type: Charm

Intonation: A-kwa ee-RUCK-toh

It is a water making spell that produces a jet of clean drinkable water from the caster's wand, which can be controlled by the user.

Seen: Used many times to extinguish fires in 1994.

Etymology: Aqua means water in Latin. Eructo is a verb meaning "I raise".

Amato Animo Animato Animagus

> **Type:** Transfiguration
>
> **Intonation:** ah-MAH-toh ah-NEE-moh ah-nee-MAH-toh an-a-MAY-jus

It is a transfiguration spell used as a part of the process of becoming Anigamus- a witch or wizard with the rare ability to transform into a particular animal at will. The spell is very dangerous to perform and all users are required to be registered by the Ministry of magic.

Etymology: Overall, the incantation can roughly mean "My love brings me life, I am obliged to become an animal wizard."

Aparecium

> **Type:** Charm
>
> **Intonation:** AH-par-EE-see-um

It is a revealing spell which reveals secret messages written in invisible ink, or any other hidden markings, the spell also works against concealing charms.

Seen: Used (to no avail) in 1993 by Hermione Granger to attempt to reveal any hidden writing in a diary.

Etymology: Latin apparere, meaning "to appear"; -ium and -cium are common Latin noun endings.

Appare Vestigium

Type: Charm

Intonation: ah-PAR-ay ves-TEE-jee-um

It is a tracking spell that reveals traces of magic, including footprints and track marks.

Seen: Newton Scamander used it to search for Porpentina Goldstein

Apparition

Type: Transportation

It is a transportation spell that magically transports the caster to another location instantaneously. The location has to be visited or seen by the primary user previously. It can be used to transport multiple people at once if holding each other.

Seen: Used several times by several people. In year six, Dumbledore uses it to take Harry to visit Slughorn. The seventh year, Hermione, Ron and Harry use it while searching for the horcruxes.

Arania Exumai

Type: Charm

Intonation: ah-RAHN-ee-a EKS-su-may

It is a spell which is used to drive away spiders, including Acromantulas-giant magical species of Spider.

Seen: Jacob's brother used this spell to repel an Acromantula that protected the Forest Vault in the Forbidden Forest.

Etymology: From the Latin aranea means "spider", and exuo means "I lay aside".

DIMINUENDO

Type: Charm

Intonation: dim-in-YEW-en-DOUGH

This spell forces the targeted object or victim to shrink in size.

Seen: Performed by Nigel Wolpert in 1995.

Etymology: The spell derives from the musical term diminuendo,meaning "a gradual decrease of the volume of sound".

ENGORGIO

Type: Charm

Intonation: en-GOR-jee-oh

A spell that causes an object to increase in size.

Seen: Rubeus Hagrid used this spell on his pumpkins in 1992; Two years later, Barty Crouch Jr cast this spell on a spider for students to see more easily when he cast a curse on him. Used in another spider three years later to test a new wand.

Etymology: The English word engorge means "swell".

CALVORIO

> **Type**: Curse
>
> **Intonation**: cal-VOR-ee-oh

A magical spell that removes the victim's hair.

Seen: The book Curses and against curses of Vindictus Viridian mentions this curse.

Etymology: From Latin calvus = "bald".

CAPACIOUS EXTREMIS

> **Intonation**: ca-PAY-shus ex-TREEM-us
>
> **Type**: Charm

 A spell which expands the internal dimensions of an object without affecting the external dimensions, rendering its contents lighter and enhancing its capacity.

Seen: Arthur Weasley used this spell to allow eight people, six large trunks, two owls and a rat to comfortably fit inside his modified Ford Anglia in 1992. Also, in the store where the Weasleys, Harry and Hermione stay during the World Quidditch Cup in 1994; Harry, Ron and Hermione also used the store as a shelter in 1997. In addition, Hermione cast this spell on her purse in the same year.

CARPE RETRACTUM

Type: Charm

Intonation: CAR-pay ruh-TRACK-tum

A magical spell which produces a rope of light to pull objects towards the caster, or to pull the caster towards the target if it's attached or fixed to a certain place.

Seen: In 1993 and 1994 by Harry Potter and Ron Weasley.

Etymology: From the Latin carpe means "to seize" and retracto means "I draw back".

CIRCUMROTA

Type: Charm

Intonation: SIR-cum-roh-tuh

A spell which can rotate objects.

Seen: This spell was used by Leta Lestrange to rotate a tower of records in the Record Room at the headquarters of the French Ministry of Magic, revealing that Newton Scamander and Porpentina Goldstein were hiding behind the tower.

COLLOPORTUS

Type: Charm

Intonation: cul-loh-POR-tus

A counter- charm to the unlocking spell, this spell can lock doors or any object that can be locked. The only spell which can counter this spell is "Alohomora".

Seen: Used by Hermione in 1996 in an attempt to prevent the Death Eaters that were following her from catching up.

Etymology: Perhaps a portmanteau of the Latin words colligere, which means "gather" and porta, which means "gate".

COLLOSHOO

Type: Hex

Intonation: CAWL-low-shoo

The spell caster can use this spell to stick the target's shoes to the ground while he or she is wearing.

Seen: This spell is mentioned twice, once it has been used in Severus Snape during a potion class, the other when Vindictus Viridian reads Curses and Against Curses.

Etymology: The suffix "shoo" is a phonetic spelling of English "shoe"; the prefix collo may come from Greek "κολάω,κολώ" (pronounced "colas","cols"), which means "to glue".

CRINUS MUTO

Type: Transfiguration

This spell is used to transfigure the style and color of one's hair.

Seen: This maybe be the spell that causes Harry potter to turn his eyebrow yellow in 1996.

DEFODIO

Type: Charm

Intonation: deh-FOH-dee-oh

This spell allows the caster to carve or dig through a target.

Seen: Used by The Trio to escape from a bank in 1998 while riding a dragon. He was later used by Harry to write Dobby's epitaph, who had been killed.

Etymology: The incantation is Latin for "I dig".

DRACONIFORS

Type: Transfiguration

Intonation: drah-KOH-nih-fors

This transfiguration spell is used to transform the target into a dragon.

Seen: Used many times in 1993 and 1994.

Etymology: From the Latin word draco, meaning "dragon", and forma meaning "shape".

DUCKLIFORS

Type: Transfiguration, Jinx

Intonation: DUCK-lih-fors

A transfiguration spell which transforms the targeted person into a duck.

Etymology: From the English duck, and the Latin forma meaning "shape".

Seen: Many times in 1994 and 1995.

EBUBLIO

Type: Jinx

Intonation: ee-BUB-lee-oh

This spell can be used to inflate and explode the target into hundreds of bubbles, but can only be cast if an ally or friend is using Aqua Eructo on the targeted person at the same time.

Seen: Used multiple times in 1994.

EPOXIMISE

Type: Transfiguration

Intonation: ee-POX-i-mise

A transfiguration spell which adheres one object to another as if they are glued together which can also lead to permanent sticking.

Seen: Students often use this spell to adhere their belongings to their desks (or, unfortunately, to their hands).

Etymology: Epoximise comes from the English word epoxy, which is a type of adhesive.

ENGORGIO SKULLUS

Type: Hex

Intonation: in-GORE-jee-oh SKUH-las

This spell is a variation of the Engorgement charm, it causes the targeted person's skull to swell disproportionately.

Seen: This spell can be purchased at Wiseacres Wizarding Equipment in Diagon Alley.

Etymology: See etymology for above entry; "skullus" is Latin for "skull".

ENTOMORPHIS

Type: Jinx, Transfiguration

Intonation: en-TOE-morph-is

For a short period of time, the targeted person transforms into an insectoid under this spell.

Seen: Harry Potter contemplated using this spell against Dudley Dursley in 1995, although he decided not to.

Everte Statum

Type: Spell

Intonation: ee-VER-tay STAH-tum

This spell is used to throw the targeted person backward. Used by Draco Malfoy on Harry Potter during the Dueling Club.

Seen: Draco Malfoy used this spell on Harry Potter in 1992 during the Dueling Club.

Etymology: The Latin words everte, which means "to throw out" and statua, from the same language, meaning "image".

Fianto Duri

Type: Charm

Intonation: fee-AN-toh DOO-ree

It is a defensive spell that strengthens shield spells or other objects to protect oneself.

Seen: Used to protect a school in 1998.

Etymology: Latin fiant means "become" and duri means "hard".

Finestra

Type: Charm

A spell that shatters glass.

Seen: On December 6, 1926, Newt Scamander broke the front window of Voclain & Co. jewelry in New York using this spell to try to recover his escaped niffler when he saw him loose inside the store stealing things.

FLINTIFORS

Type: Transfiguration

Intonation: FLINT-i-fors

A transfiguration spell which transforms objects into matchboxes.

Seen: In the 1980s, this spell was covered in third-year transfiguration classes.

Notes: This may be related to, or the incantation for Match to needle. This spell was originally cut from Harry Potter and the Philosopher's Stone (video game) for the PC, but was brought back for Harry Potter: Hogwarts Mystery.

FLIPENDO

Type: Jinx

Intonation: fli-PEN-doh

A spell taught in defense against the dark arts, it can knock creatures or objects backward.

Flipendo Tria

Type: Jinx

Intonation: flih-PEN-doh TREE-ah

This spell is a more powerful version of Flipendo and resembles a miniature tornado.

Seen: In 1991 and 1993.

Fumos

Type: Charm

Intonation: FYOO-moss

A spell used to create a defensive smokescreen that hinders visibility.

Seen: This spell, used in 1993, is covered in The Dark Forces: A Guide to Self-Protection.

Furnunclus

Type: Jinx

Intonation: fer-NUN-kyoo-luss

A spell that covers the targeted person with pimples or boils.

Seen: Used by Harry Potter on Gregory Goyle.

Etymology: Latin furnunculus, meaning "petty thief", or English furuncle, a synonym for "boil".

Glacius

> **Type:** Charm
>
> **Intonation:** GLAY-see-us

A freezing spell which freezes the target with icy-cold air. A bit different from the Freezing charm which merely immobilizes things.

Seen: Used in video games from Harry Potter and the Prisoner of Azkaban (video game).

Etymology: From Latin glacies, which means "ice".

Notes: Not to be confused with the Freezing Charm, which merely immobilises things.

Gytrash

> **Type:** Conjuration, Dark Arts

A conjuring spell which conjures luminous green Gytrashes (legendary black dogs) from the wand, the caster can command the gytrash to attack an opponent.

Harmonia Nectere Passus

Intonation: har-MOH-nee-a NECK-teh-ray PASS-us

Type: Charm

A spell used to repair a Vanishing Cabinet.

Seen: Used by Draco Malfoy to mend a cabinet in 1996.

Etymology: Latin harmonia, which means "harmony", nectere, which means "to bind", and passus, which means "step".

Herbifors

Type: Transfiguration

It is a transfiguration spell that causes flowers to sprout from the victim.

Seen: It may be bought at Wiseacre's Wizarding Equipment.

Herbivicius

Type: Charm

Intonation: her-BIV-i-cuss

It is a spell used to rapidly grows plants.

Seen: In the 1994–1995 school year, not in books or movies.

HOMENUM REVELIO

Type: Charm

Intonation: HOM-eh-num reh-VEH-lee-oh

Description: Shows the presence of humans near the caster.

Seen: Used many times by various people in 1997.

Etymology: Most likely from Latin homo means human, and "reveal", though the classical Latin form would be hominem instead of homenum, which shows Portuguese influence — indeed, Rowling speaks the language.

HORCRUX MAKING SPELL

Type: Dark Arts

One of the most powerful spells that allow a part of a wizard's soul to pass into a chosen object, which makes the chosen object a Horcrux. To make this spell successful, one has to commit murder and take advantage of the soul's "splitting apart" using this supreme act of evil in order to be able to perform this spell, making it one of the most complex spell. This secret spell was used by Lord Voldemort while creating his Horcruxes.

Seen: Used by Lord Voldemort while creating his Horcruxes.

Notes: When JK Rowling was asked about the steps to create a Horcrux Rowling, he refused to answer, saying "some things are better left unsaid." However, in the Harry Potter Encyclopedia, it is explained, and it is said that the editor felt like vomiting after reading it.

ILLEGIBILUS

Type: Charm

Intonation: i-LEDJ-i-bull-is

This spell is used to make a writing impossible to read.

INANIMATUS CONJURUS

Type: Transfiguration

Intonation: in-an-ih-MAH-tus CON-jur-us

It is transfiguration spell used to conjure an inanimate object.

Seen: Mentioned briefly in 1995.

INCENDIO DUO

Type: Charm

Intonation: in-SEN-dee-oh DOO-oh

It is the stronger version of the spell "Incendio" which is used to produce fire.

Seen: It was in Harry Potter and the Chamber of Secrets (GBC)

INCENDIO TRIA

Type: Charm

Intonation: in-SEN-dee-oh TREE-ah

This spell is the strongest version of "Incendio" which is used to produce fire.

Seen: It was in Harry Potter and the Philosopher's Stone (video game), Harry Potter and the Chamber of Secrets (video game) and Harry Potter and the Prisoner of Azkaban (video game).

INFLATUS

Type: Charm

Intonation: in-FLAY-tus

It is a spell used to inflate the target filling it with air.

Seen: Watch on Harry Potter and the prisoner of Azkaban and Harry Potter and the Goblet of Fire (video game)

Etymology: The prefix 'Inflate' derives from the English verb "to expand with oxygen".

LOCOMOTOR WIBBLY

It is a spell used to make the victim's legs collapse as if they were turned into jelly.

Type: Charm

Intonation: la-KAR-num in-flah-MAR-ee

It is a spell that ignites the cloak of the targeted person. Hermione once used this spell to set Snape's cloak on fire to stop him from cursing Harry.

Seen: Used by Hermione in 1991 to prevent Snape from cursing Harry. Enchantment is only used in the film adaptation of Harry Potter and the philosopher's stone.

Etymology: Latin inflammo, or the verb inflammatio meaning "to set on fire". Lacarnum, from the Latin "lacerna", meaning "cloak".

Type: Transfiguration

Intonation: LAP-ih-forz

A transfiguration spell that transforms the targeted person into a rabbit.

Seen: Used by Hermione in the video games Harry Potter and the Prisoner of Azkaban and Harry Potter and the goblet of fire.

Etymology: From Latin lepus meaning hare, and forma meaning "shape".

LUMOS DUO

Type: Charm

Intonation: LOO-mos DOO-oh

It is a more powerful version of Lumos, it is used to create a focused beam of light from the tip of the caster's wand.

Seen: Learned and used by Ron in the adaptation of the video game of Harry Potter and the Prisoner of Azkaban.

Etymology: Lumos plus Latin duo, "two".

LUMOS SOLEM

Type: Charm

Intonation: LOO-mos SO-lem

This spell is the ultimate version of Lumos, it produces a blinding flash of sunlight that can blind anyone for a few moments. The spell is used to conjure Sunlight.

Seen: Used by Hermione to free Ron from the devil's trap. The enchantment was only used in the film adaptation of Harry Potter and the philosopher's stone.

Etymology: Derived from two words; the Latin lumen, meaning "light", and the Latin word for "sun", which in its accusative case is "solem".

MAGICUS EXTREMOS

Type: Charm

It is a spell which needs to collaborate with a partner that helps to temporarily increase the caster's spell power.

MELOFORS

Type: Jinx

It is a spell used to encase the targeted person's head in a pumpkin.

Seen: It was rumored that Cornelius Fudge had been a victim of this evil eye after being defeated by Albus Dumbledore in a duel in 1996.

METELOJINX RECANTO

Type: Counter-Charm

Intonation: mee-tee-OH-loh-jinks reh-CAN-toh.

It is a counter-spell which causes other spells made on the weather effects, to cease.

Seen: Suggested in 1997 by Arthur Weasley to Ron (disguised as Reginald Cattermole through the use of multiplayer potion) as the best way to clear the curse of rain in an office of the Ministry. Also used by Bartemius Crouch Jr (disguised as Alastor Moody) in 1994 to cease the climatic effect of the Great Hall's ceiling insisting that it is broken when he told Dumbledore to "fix his roof."

Etymology: Meteorology, the study of weather, the word jinx and recant, "to withdraw or retract". Interestingly in modern English recant means to say that you no longer hold a belief.

MOLLIARE

Type: Charm

Intonation: mull-ee-AR-ay

It is a spell mostly used in the manufacturing of broomsticks; it produces an invisible cushion over the target. Hermione Granger used it on Ron and Harry to cushion their fall in Gringotts Wizard Bank. This spell is similar to Spongify and Arresto Momentum.

Seen: Used by Hermione Granger to cushion the fall of her, Harry and Ron at the Gringotts Wizard Bank in 1998.

Notes: This spell may be related to Arresto Momentum and Spongify.

MOLLY WEASLEY'S CURSE

A spell that caused Bellatrix's death, it is similar to Avada Kedavra; as it kills or freezes the targeted person. The body then turns greenish blue slowly turning into stone. This spell, when accompanied with another jinx can blast the body into pieces.

Seen: Molly Weasley used the curse after Bellatrix Lestrange attacked Ginny Weasley. It is only used in the film version.

Notes: This may be Duro or a Freezing Charm, although the latter is shown to be blue in 1992.

MORSMORDRE

Intonation: morz-MOR-druh

It is a spell that conjures the Dead mark which is the sign of the Death Eaters. It was invented by Lord Voldemort and was used to lure Albus Dumbledore to his death.

Seen: Used by Barty Crouch Jr in 1994. Also seen in 1997 over the castle to attract Albus Dumbledore to his death. Apparently it was invented by Lord Voldemort.

Etymology: Latin mors, "death", and mordere, meaning "to bite" (or its French derivative mordre); this would appear to be associated with the name of Lord Voldemort's followers, the Death Eaters. The English murder might also contribute.

MUCUS AD NAUSEAM

Type: Curse

Intonation: MYOO-kus ahd NAW-zee-um

A spell that gives the targeted person an extremely runny nose and a nasty cold accompanied with constant sneezing which can also cause the victim to collapse or become unconscious.

Seen: Mentioned by Professor Quirrell to his first-year class.

MULTICORFORS

Type: Transfiguration

Intonation: mull-tee-COR-fors

It is a transfiguration spell that is used to change the style and color of the targeted person's clothing.

Seen: It may also be the same charm as when Harry accidentally changed the color of his eyebrow, before inviting Luna to the Slughorn Christmas party. (It is unlikely, since it was performed as a Transfiguration exercise, which is not related to Charms.) It could possibly have been used when Harry accidentally changed the color of his teachers' hair at St. Grogory Elementary School.

Mutatio Skullus

Type: Hex

Intonation: myoo-TAY-toh SKULL-us

It is a spell used to mutate the head of the victim causing them to grow extra heads.

Seen: Used by the ancient Egyptian magicians, as noted by Ron Weasley in 1993.

Nebulus

Type: Charm

Intonation: NEH-bu-lus

It is a spell that creates fog from the tip of the wand. It is also an incantation for the Ministry of the Magic Fog.

Seen: In 1927, Albus Dumbledore used this spell to conjure a fog in London to provide concealment for his meeting with Newton Scamander.

Notes: This may be the incantation for the Ministry of Magic Fog.

OCULUS REPARO

Type: Charm

It is a spell used to mend eyeglasses. It is used by Hermione many a time to fix Harry's glasses.

Seen: Used by Hermione in 1991 and 1992 to fix Harry's glasses.

Notes: This spell is a variation of Reparo.

OBLITERATION

Type: Charm

It is a charm used to remove footprints.

Seen: Used by Hermione in 1995 to eliminate the traces that she, Harry and Ron left in the snow as they walked towards Hagrid's cabin. Also used in 1997 by Hermione to remove the traces she and Harry left behind them in the snow while traveling through Godric's Hollow.

Notes: The previous instance in book five only reveals that the obliteration spell can eliminate traces. There is no explanation about what effect it can have on other things. He could possibly destroy things, according to his name.

OPPUGNO

Type: Jinx

Intonation: oh-PUG-noh

Makes specific objects attack a victim. It is particularly effective in conjunction with the conjuring spell of birds.

Seen: Used by Hermione in 1996 to attack Ron with a summoned flock of canaries during an argument.

Etymology: Latin oppugno, "I attack"

ORBIS

Type: Jinx

Intonation: OR-biss

It is a spell that sucks the targeted object or person into the ground.

Seen: Used many times in 1993.

Etymology: Orbis is Latin for 'circle', which reflects the spell's physical appearance.

OSCAUSI

Type: Dark charm

Intonation: os-SCOW-zee

It is a dark charm that seals the targeted person's mouth shut making it look like it was never there.

Seen: Used by Leta Lestrange in a Gryffindor girl when they were both in their third year at Hogwarts. The Gryffindor girl was speaking badly of Lestrange behind her back until Lestrange left her near hiding place and silenced the Gryffindor girl with this spell.

Etymology: Possibly derived as a portmanteau of os, Latin for "mouth", and clausi for "I shut". It may additionally be a pun or wordplay on scusi, the Italian interjection for "excuse me".

PACK

Type: Charm

A spell used to pack luggage.

Seen: Used in Harry Potter and the Prisoner of Azkaban by Remus Lupine in his office, and in Harry Potter and the Order of the Phoenix by Nymphadora Tonks, once verbally and again not verbally.

PAPYRUS REPARO

Type: Charm

It is a spell used to mend torn pieces of paper and also a variation of Reparo.

Seen/Mentioned: This spell was used by Newton Scamander in 1927 to restore a torn postcard of Porpentina Goldstein addressed to Queenie Goldstein.

Notes: This spell is a variation of Reparo.

Partis Temporus

Type: Charm

Intonation: PAR-tis temp-OAR-us

It is a spell used to create a temporary gap in the targeted space. In Half-Blood Prince, Professor Albus Dumbledore used it so that he and Harry can pass through the ring of fire used to ward off the Inferi.

Seen: Used by Albus Dumbledore in Crystal Cave in the film adaptation of Harry Potter and the mystery of the prince. He uses it so that he and Harry can go through the ring of fire used to protect themselves from the Inferi.

Etymology: Partis is a plural form of the French verb partir, which means "to separate," "to go away," "to leave," or "to depart." Temporis is Latin for "time."

Peskipiksi Pesternomi

Type: Charm

Intonation: PES-key PIX-ee PES-ter NO-mee

The uses of this spell haven't been discovered yet, it was used once but had absolutely no effect.

Seen: Used by Lockhart to try to remove Cornish Pixies.

Etymology: English pesky meaning "annoying", English pixie meaning "a supernatural being", English pester meaning "to annoy", English no for negative and English me for the first person pronoun.

PISCIFORS

Type: Transfiguration

It is a transfiguration spell to transform the target into a fish.

Seen: He appeared in Harry Potter and the Goblet of Fire (video game) and mentioned in Harry Potter and the Half-Blood Prince (film).

PRIOR INCANTATO

Type: Charm

Intonation: pri-OR in-can-TAH-toh

It is a spell used to force a wand to show an "echo" of the last spell it performed.

Seen: Used by Amos Diggory in 1994 to discover the last spell cast by Harry's wand after it was found in the hands of Winky, a house elf.

Etymology: Latin prior, "previous", and incantare, "to speak a spell" (past participle incantatum).

Notes: Can manifest in the form of the Reverse Spell effect, or Priori Incantatem, when wands with the same core attempt to do battle.

PROTEGO DIABOLICA

Type: Charm

Intonation: pro-TAY-goh

It is a conjuring spell which conjures a protective ring of black fire around the caster of the spell which can only affect their enemies.

Seen: First seen in 1995, in which Hermione teaches Harry this spell in preparation for the third task in the Three Wizard Tournament. Albus Dumbledore uses a similar spell that reverses the construction of glass in sand when Voldemort sent shards of glass to try to stab Dumbledore. Fred and George Weasley loved the hats they called "shield hats" with this spell in 1997.

Etymology: Latin protego, "I cover" or "I protect".

REDACTUM SKULLUS

Type: Hex

Intonation: reh-DAK-tum SKULL-us

It is a head-shrink spell that shrinks the head of the targeted person, a counter-spell to Engorgio Skullus.

REPARIFORS

Type: Healing Spell

Intonation: re-PAR-i-fors

It is a spell used to revert minor magically induced ailments such as poisoning or paralysis.

Seen: Harry Potter and the Prisoner of Azkaban (video game)

REVERTE

Type: Charm

Intonation: ree-VUHR-tay

It is a spell used to return objects to their original states or positions.

Seen: Record Room of the Ministry of Magic of France at the headquarters of the Ministry of Magic of France, in an attempt to flee from chasing Matagots. This sent all the record towers, previously summoned by Lestrange, flying back and returning to their original positions on the ground.

Etymology: Reverte is derived from Latin for "you shall return", being a second-person imperative form (singular, present, active) of the verb reverto ("I return, or turn back").

REPARIFARGE

Type: Untransfiguration

Intonation: reh-PAR-i-farj

It is an untransfiguration spell used to reverse incomplete transformations.

Seen: Seen only so far in the Beginner's Guide to the Transfiguration in Pottermore.

Etymology: This information is currently unknown.

REPELLO INIMICUM

> **Type:** Charm

> **Intonation:** ruh-PEL-oh MUH-guhl-tuhm

It is a spell used to disintegrate snatchers.

Seen: Mentioned in Quidditch Through the Ages as used to keep Muggles out of the Quidditch World Cup. It was also said that Hogwarts was guarded by the spell that repels muggles. It was also used by Harry and Hermione on numerous occasions, among many other spells, to protect and hide their camp in 1997.

SCORCHING SPELL

> **Type:** Charm

It is a fiery offensive spell that produces dancing flames to scorch the opponent.

Seen: Professor McGonagall used this spell on Snape in 1998.

SEALANT CHARM

> **Type:** Charm

It is a spell used to magically seal envelopes.

Seen: The Magical Congress of the United States of America required all applicants for wand permits in the United States to close the envelope in which they sent their applications to the Wand Permits Office with this spell.

Notes: This may be the parchment-sealing spell that Dolores Umbridge used in 1995.

SHIELD PENETRATION SPELL

Type: Spell

Intonation: unknown

This spell is used to annihilate magical shields and enchantments.

Seen: Used by Voldemort to break the enchantments placed around the Hogwarts School of Witchcraft and Wizardry in 1998 by Filius Flitwick, Minerva McGonagall and Molly Weasley.

Etymology: unknown

SKURGE

Type: Charm

Intonation: SKURJ

It is a spell used to frighten ghosts and other spirits and to clean up ectoplasm.

Seen: The video game Harry Potter and the secret chamber. Harry finds it in a spell book in the Restricted Section of the Hogwarts Library (possibly misfiled) and uses it to clean the doors and treasure chests that have been shed by malevolent ghosts.

SPECIALIS REVELIO

Type: Charm

Intonation: spe-see-AL-is reh-VEL-ee-oh

It is a charm used to reveal spells that had been cast on potions or objects.

Seen: Used by Hermione Granger to get more information about the Harry's Advanced Potion-Making book in 1996. Used by Ernie Macmillan to discover the ingredients of a potion.

Etymology: Latin specialis, "particular;individual" and revelare (present tense revelo), "unveil".

SPONGIFY

Type: Charm

Intonation: SPUN-ji-fye

It is a spell used to make the texture of the targeted object soft, making them bouncy and rubbery.

Seen: This charm is seen in The Book of Spells, Grade 1 on Pottermore.

SQUIGGLE QUILL

Type: Transfiguration

It is a transfiguration spell used to transform writing quills into worms.

Seen: The only appearance was in the Harry Potter collectible card game.

Notes: This spell may be Vermiculus.

STEALTH SPONSORING SPELL

Type: Spell

A spell used to detect people or objects who are under magical disguise.

Seen: In 1996, Professor Umbridge cast this around her office.

STELEUS

Type: Hex

It is a spell that makes the targeted person sneeze for a short period of time. It is used during duels to distract the opponent.

Seen: It is only seen in Harry Potter and the Prisoner of Azkaban (video game).

Etymology: Steleus derives from the Latin sternuo means I sneeze.

SUPERSENSORY CHARM

Type: Charm

It is a spell which grants the caster enhanced senses so that they can sense things they would not normally see or feel.

Seen: Mentioned by Ron outside the Hogwarts Express in 2017 as a possible substitute for using mirrors while driving a Muggle mobile car.

SURGITO

Type: Counter-charm

Intonation: SUR-jee-toh

This spell is a counterspell used to remove enchantments placed on people or objects.

Seen: In 1927, Newton Scamander used Surgito to lift an enchantment that was placed on Jacob Kowalski. As a result of the spell, Kowalski woke up from the enchanted state of reverie and regained consciousness of reality in the present.

Etymology: Surgito is a Latin word in the imperative form meaning "you/he/she shall arise, or get up", and is a conjugation of the verb surgo ("I arise"). The etymology is appropriate, considering that the effects of the spell on Jacob Kowalski can be likened to waking up from a confused, dreamlike state.

SWITCHING SPELL

Type: Transfiguration

It is a transfiguration spell used to switch positions between two targets simultaneously.

Seen: Harry contemplated using this spell against his dragon in the first task of the Triwizard Tournament. ((He considered changing his fangs for wine gums)). Neville Longbottom misuses the spell, transplanting his ears to a cactus.

Tabboo

> **Type:** Curse

It is a spell which can be placed on words or a name, when the name or the word is spoken, a disturbance is created which alerts the caster of the spell, and lets him or her know the location of the speaker. Protective enchantments which are in effect around the speaker of the word or name are all broken when the tabooed word is spoken. This spell was placed on the name "Voldemort".

Seen: In Deathly Hallows, this spell is placed on the word "Voldemort"; Harry, Ron and Hermione are tracked this way to Tottenham Court Road. Ron tells the other two to stop using the word, as he began to fear that the name could be an evil eye, and then discovered that it was a taboo. Later in the book, Harry accidentally says Voldemort's name again, resulting in the trio being caught by Death Eaters and taken to Malfoy Manor.

Tail Growing Hex

> **Type:** Hex

It is a spell which causes the targeted person to grow a tail.

Seen: When Miranda Goshawk had her Book of Spells printed, she gave copies to her sisters that had various misprints in them; one such misprint somehow gave her sister Romilda a tail. Timothy Blenkinsop was hit with this hex when he was caught in the crossfire of a Puddlemere United vs. Holyhead Harpies riot.

TEACUP TO TORTOISE

Type: Transfiguration

It is a transfiguration spell which transforms a teacup into a tortoise.

Seen: Seen on the Scholastic Harry Potter Official Site.

Notes: It may be related to the Teapot spell for turtle covered in the third year at the Hogwarts School of Witchcraft and Wizardry.

TEAPOT TO TORTOISE

Type: Transfiguration

A transfiguration spell which transforms a teapot into a tortoise.

Seen: Third years at the Hogwarts School of Witchcraft and Wizardry were required to cast the spell during their final exams.

Notes: May be related to the teapot to Teacup to tortoise spell.

TEETH STRAIGHTENING SPELL

Type: Charm

A spell that straightens crooked teeth.

Seen: Sir Nicholas of Mimsy-Porpington tried to use this spell on Lady Grieve at his request, but failed and gave him a fang. He was executed the next morning. After he returned as a ghost, Nick Almost Beheaded recounted the incident in a ballad.

TELEPORTATION SPELL

Type: Spell

A spell used to teleport an object or a person to another destination.

Seen: In 1996, Albus Dumbledore used this to transport Harry Potter's school supplies, clothes, and owl to the Burrow.

TENTACLIFORS

Type: Transfiguration, Jinx

It is a transfiguration spell that transfigures the targeted person's head into a tentacle.

TERGEO

Type: Charm

Intonation: TUR-jee-oh

It is a spell used to clean objects or draws off liquid.

Seen: Hermione Granger used the spell in 1996 to remove blood from Harry's face. It is later used to remove spilled ink from the parchment. It was also used in 1997 to clean a Ron handkerchief and dust off a photo of Gellert Grindelwald in the house of Bathilda Bagshot of Harry Potter.

Etymology: Latin tergere, "wipe off; cleanse".

TITILLANDO

Type: Hex

Intonation: ti-tee-LAN-do

It is a spell used to weaken a victim by tickling him. Mostly used as a method to torture someone.

Seen: Harry Potter Trading Card Game, later seen in spells/duels on Pottermore.

TRANSMOGRIFIAN TORTURE

Type: Curse

It is a dangerous spell that is used to torture the victim to death.

Seen: Gilderoy Lockhart suggested that it was this curse that "killed" Mrs. Norris after she was actually found petrified on a torch bracket.

Etymology: English "transmogrify", meaning "to change or alter greatly, often to grotesque effect", possibly implying that the curse changes the shape of the victim to cause pain.

Notes: The incantation to this curse is possibly Transmogrify.

TWITCHY-EARS HEX

> **Type**: Hex

A spell which makes the victim's ears twitch.

Seen: Miranda Goshawk recommended that this be for someone who practices the shield spell.

Notes:. During the fourth year Hex-deflection test for Defence Against the Dark Arts, Harry Potter was hexed with this spell by Bartemius Crouch Junior (then disguised as Alastor Moody).

UNBREAKABLE CHARM

> **Type**: Charm

A spell used to make the targeted object unbreakable.

Seen: Towards the end of Harry Potter and the goblet of fire, Hermione casts the spell into a jar, in which she puts Rita Skeeter in her Animagus beetle form to prevent her from becoming human.

Unbreakable Vow

Type: Spell

A spell used when a witch or wizard is taking a vow, making the vow unbreakable. The consequence of breaking the vow would be death.

Seen: Snape makes an Unbreakable Vote with Narcissa Malfoy at the beginning of the Half-Blood Prince, promising to help Narcissa's son, Draco, with a task Voldemort gave him, and finish the task in case Draco proves his disability. Fred and George tried to force an unbreakable vote on Ron as children. According to Ron, it causes death when the vote is broken.

Unsupported flight

Type: Spell

A spell that allows a wizard or witch to fly without the help of a broomstick. Lord Voldemort invented this technique.

Seen: Seen in Harry Potter and the Deathly Hallows and Harry Potter and the Cursed Child.

Vacuum Cleaner spell

Type: Charm

It is a spell used to clean objects using the wand. The wand sucks up the dust like a vacuum cleaner.

Seen: Used by Madam Malkin in 1996.

VENTUS

Type: Jinx

Intonation: VEN-tuss

It is a spell which lets the caster shoot a jet of strong spiraling wind from the tip of the wand.

Seen: Used in the video game version of Harry Potter and the Goblet of Fire.

Etymology: Ventus is a Latin word, meaning "wind".

VENTUS DUO

Type: Jinx

It is a stronger version of the spell Ventus.

Seen: In Harry Potter and the Order of the Phoenix (video game)

VERA VERTO

Type: Transfiguration

Intonation: vair-uh-VAIR-toh

It is a transfiguration spell that turns animals into water goblets. This spell was used only once in the series by Professor Minerva McGonagall during a transfiguration class she was conducting.

Seen: Used only once in the series, by Minerva McGonagall in the film adaptation of Harry Potter and the Chamber of Secrets in his Transfiguration class. Also used by Ronald Weasley without success in the same class thanks to his damaged wand.

Etymology: From Latin vera meaning "right" or "proper", and verto, meaning "I turn".

VERDILLIOUS

Type: Charm

Intonation: ver-DILL-ee-us

It is a spell that is used to shoot green sparks from the tip of the wand.

Seen: Seen in the trading card game.

Notes: This spell is most likely a typo of Verdimillious.

VERDIMILLIOUS

Type: Charm

Intonation: VERD-dee-MILL-lee-us

It is a charm that produces a jet of green sparks from the tip of the wand; it can be used during dueling for distraction and also to reveal things that are hidden by dark magic.

Seen: Learned in first-year defence against the dark arts class.

Verdimillious Duo

Type: Charm

Intonation: VERD-dee-MILL-lee-us

This spell is a more powerful version of the spell Verdimillious. This spell is taught in first-year defense against the dark art class.

Seen: Learned in first-year defence against the dark arts class.

Vermiculus

Type: Transfiguration

Intonation: vur-MICK-yoo-luhs

It is a transfiguration spell used to transform objects into worms.

Seen: Appeared in Harry Potter and the Goblet of Fire (video game).

Notes: This spell may have some connection with Squiggle Quill.

Vermillious

Type: Charm

Intonation: vur-MILL-ee-us

It is a spell that creates a jet of red sparks from the tip of the wand which can be used as a signal during a minor dueling spell or during an emergency.

Vipera Evanesca

Type: Vanishment

Intonation: vee-PAIR-uh eh-vuh-NES-kuh

It is a snake vanishing spell which is used to vanish snakes. A counter-spell to the snake summoning spell. Used at a dueling club by Severus Snape to vanish a snake summoned by Draco Malfoy while dueling Harry Porter.

Seen: Severus Snape cast this spell in 1992 at the Duel Club to vanish a snake that Draco Malfoy had conjured during a duel with Harry Potter. Albus Dumbledore also used this spell to fade the Voldemort snake during his Duel in the Atrium of the Ministry.

Etymology: Vipera is a genus of venomous vipers, a type of snake. Evanesca likely shares its origin with Evanesco, which means "disappear" in Latin.

Washing up spell

Type: Charm

It is a spell that makes dirty dishes wash themselves.

Seen: Molly Weasley used it nonverbally after preparing breakfast for Harry Potter upon arrival at The Burrow on August 4, 1992.

Type: Charm

It is a spell that produces a jet of white spark which can be used offensively during a minor dueling spell.

Seen: After the victory of the American national Quidditch team in the semifinals of the 2014 Quidditch World Cup against Liechtenstein, the red, white and blue sparks filled the air so densely that it was difficult to see or breathe.

Notes: The incantation to this spell is almost certainly Baubillious.

ANTI-DISAPPARITON JINX

Type: Jinx

It is a spell which can be cast by the user to prevent Disapparition (teleportation) within a certain area.

Seen: Used by Albus Dumbledore to catch some Death Eaters in the Department of Mysteries in 1996. I also mentioned that no one can disappear from Hogwarts; It is due to this curse.

ANTI-INTRUDER JINX

Type: Jinx

It is a spell used to repel intruders from homes or private properties.

Seen: He was placed at Hogwarts School of Witchcraft and Wizardry in 1996 for additional protection during a Death Eater invasion.

BACKFIRING JINX

It is a spell used to cause the spells to backfire and hurt its caster.

BITING JINX

This spell causes jinxed objects to bite the user.

BROOM JINX

It is a spell that makes a broomstick attempt to throw its rider off.

Seen: It was used by Quirinus Quirrell against Harry Potter in 1991.

Notes: This may be related to the Hurling Hex.

ORBIS JINX

It is a spell that makes the ground suck in the targeted person.

Seen: Used multiple times in 1993.

Etymology: Orbis is Latin for 'circle', which reflects the spell's physical appearance.

CONJUNCTIVITIS CURSE

It is a spell that causes irritation in the targeted person's eye. The victim's eyes swell shut like an eye infection called conjunctivitis.

Seen: Sirius Black suggested in his letter to Harry potter to use this spell on a dragon. Olympe Maxime used this spell on some giants in 1995.

Etymology: "Conjunctivitis" is the technical term for "pink eye," demonstrating its effects of irritating the eye and causing it to shut.

FLAGRANTE CURSE

It is a spell that causes the targeted object to emit heat whenever it is touched by a person.

Seen: The Vault of Lestrange had this curse.

FULL BODY BIND CURSE

It is a curse that instantly paralyzes the targeted person. Used mostly during dueling.

GORMLAITH GAUNT'S CURSE

It is one of the most powerful spells which puts the targeted person into an enchanted slumber from which he/she can hardly wake up.

ANTI-CHEATING SPELL

This spell was used at Hogwarts School of Wizardry and Witchcraft on parchments or writing quills so as to prevent the students from cheating during exams and classes.

Antonin Dolohov's Curse

It is a curse that inflicts injuries on the targeted person, injuries capable enough to kill someone.

Seen/Mentioned: Used by Antonin Dolohov during the Battle of the Department of Mysteries twice; Dolohov was under a silencer spell, and therefore weakened the effects of this curse, saving Hermione from death, but incapacitated her and demanded that she take ten potions a day for some time.

Badgering

It is a transfiguration spell that turns things into badgers.

Seen/Mentioned: Appeared in Harry Potter and the Chamber of Secrets and Harry Potter Trading Card Game.

Bat–Bogey Hex

It is a transfiguration spell that transforms the targeted person's bogeys into large bats that fly out of his or her nose. Miranda Goshawk invented this spell.

Seen/Mentioned: Ginny Weasley was a noted practitioner of this spell, having used it at least thrice by her sixth year.

Bedazzling Hex

It is a spell that allows the person casting the spell disguise things, most of the cloaks of invisibility are made with this spell.

Seen: When Xenophilius Lovegood explains the concept of how the Invisibility Cloak is the only thing that can make a person truly invisible, he mentions that most layers of that type are made with this spell.

Note: Although the exact effects are unknown, depending on the name (and the fact that it is used together with a chameleon charm in certain layers, it is probably used to hide a person or object.

BEWITCHED SNOWBALLS

It is a spell that causes snowballs to pelt themselves at the target.

Seen: Twice used by Fred and George Weasley; first on the head of Professor Quirrell, involuntarily hitting Lord Voldemort in the face, and then again four years later to attack the windows of the Gryffindor Tower.

BLUEBELL FLAMES

It is a spell that produces a magical blue flame from the tip of the wand; this flame can be held in a jar. These flames are not as dangerous like actual fire and can be penetrated or touched without burning the person.

Seen: This spell was a Hermione Granger specialty. He used it to save Harry and Ron in 1991.

CHEERING CHARM

This magical spell makes the targeted person feel extremely happy. If the spell is overused on the same person then the target might break into an uncontrollable laughing fit. Felix Summerbee invented this spell.

Seen: Taught to third-year charms classes, part of the written O.W.L.

List of Spell A to Z

Spell list of "A"

Aberto

Accio (Summoning Charm)

Age Line

Aguamenti (Water-Making Spell)

Alarte Ascendare

Albus Dumbledore's Forceful Spell

Alohomora (Opening Charm).

Anapneo.

Anteoculatia.

Anti-Jinx.

Anti-Cheating Spell.

Anti-Disapparition Jinx.

Antonin Dolohov's curse.

Aparecium (Exposing Charm).

Appare Vestigium.

Apparate.

Aqua Eructo (Aqua Eructo Charm).

Arania Exumai.

Arresto Momentum

Arrow-shooting spell.

Ascendio.

Avada Kedavra (Eliminating Curse).

Avifors (Avifors Spell).

Avis (Bird-Conjuring Charm).

Spell list of "B"

Bat-Bogey Hex.

Baubillious.

Babbling Curse

Bedazzling Hex.

Bewitched Snowballs.

Bluebell Blazes.

Bombarda.

Bombarda Maxima.

Brackium Emendo.

Bubble-Head Charm.

Bubble-producing spell.

Spell list of "C"

Calvario (Hair-Loss Curse).

Cantis.

Carpe Retractum (Take as well as Draw Charm).

Cascading Jinx.

Caterwauling Charm.

Cauldron to Sieve

Cave Inimicum.

Cheering Appeal.

Cistem Aperio.

Colloportus (Locking Spell).

Colloshoo (Stickfast Hex).

Colovaria (Colour Change Charm).

Confringo (Blowing Up Curse).

Confundo (Confundus Charm).

Conjunctivitis Curse.

Cornflake skin spell.

Cracker Jinx

Cribbing Spell

Crinus Muto

Crucio (Cruciatus Curse).

Mucus ad Nauseam (Curse of the Bogies).

Cushioning Charm.

Spell list of "D"

Defodio (Gouging Spell).

Deletrius (Removal Spell).

Densaugeo (Tooth-Growing Spell).

Depulso (Eradicating Charm).

Descendo.

Deprimo.

Diffindo (Severing Charm).

Diminuendo.

Dissendium.

Disillusionment Charm.

Draconifors (Draconifors Spell).

Drought Charm.

Ducklifors (Ducklifors Jinx).

Duro (Solidifying Charm).

Spell list of "E"

Ears to kumquats

Ear-shrivelling Curse

Ebublio (Ebublio Jinx).

Engorgio (Engorgement Appeal).

Engorgio Skullus.

Entomorphis.

Entrail-Expelling Curse.

Episkey.

Epoximise.

Erecto.

Evanesce.

Evanesco (Disappearing Spell).

Everte Statum.

Expecto Patronum (Patronus Charm).

Expelliarmus (Deactivating Charm).

Expulso (Expulso Curse).

Extinguishing spell

Eye of rabbit, harp string hum, transform this water right into rum (Transfiguration).

Spell list of "F"

Ferula.

Feather-light appeal.

Fianto Duri.

Fidelius Charm.

Fiendfyre.

Finestra.

Finite

Finite Incantatem (General Counter-Spell).

Finger-removing jinx.

Firestorm.

Flagrante Curse.

Flagrate.

Flame-Freezing Charm.

Flipendo (Knockback Jinx).

Flipendo Duo (Knockback Jinx Duo).

Flipendo Tria.

Flying Charm.

Fumos (Smokescreen Spell).

Fumos Duo.

Furnunculus (Pimple Jinx).

fur spell

Spell list of "G"

Geminio (Gemino Curse).

Glacius (Freezing Spell).

Glacius Duo.

Glacius Tria.

Glisseo.

Green Sparks.

Gripping Charm.

Spell list of "H"

Hair-thickening

Harmonia Nectere Passus.

Herbifors.

Herbivicus (Herbivicus Charm).

Hermione Granger's jinx

Homing spells.

Homenum Revelio (Human-Presence-Revealing Spell).

Homonculous Charm

Homorphus Charm

Horton-Keitch Braking Charm

Horcrux Curse

Hot-Air Charm

Hour-Reversal Charm.

Hour-Reversal Charm

Hurling Hex

Spell list of "I"

Illegibilus.

Immobulus (Icing Up Appeal).

Impedimenta (Impediment Jinx).

Imperio (Imperius Curse).

Imperturbable Charm

Impervius (Impervius Appeal).

Inanimatus Conjurus (Inanimatus Conjurus Spell).

Incarcerous.

Incendio (Fire-Making Spell)

Incendio Duo

Incendio Tria

Inflatus (Inflatus Jinx)

Informous (Informous Spell)

Intruder Charm

Locomotor Wibbly (Jelly-Legs Curse).

Spell list of "J"

Jelly-Brain Jinx

Jelly-Fingers Curse

Spell list of "K"

Knee-reversal hex

Spell list of "L"

Lacarnum Inflamarae

Langlock

Lapifors (Lapifors Spell).

Leek Jinx

Legilimens (Legilimency Spell).

Levicorpus.

Liberacorpus.

Locomotor (Mobility Charm).

Locomotor Mortis (Leg-Locker Curse).

Lumos (Wand-Lighting Charm).

Lumos Duo.

Lumos Maxima.

Lumos Solem.

Spell list of "M"

Magicus Extremos.

Melofors (Melofors Jinx).

Meteolojinx Recanto.

Mimblewimble (Tongue-Tying Curse).

Mobiliarbus.

Mobilicorpus.

Molly Weasley's Curse.

Morsmordre (Dark Mark).

Muffliato (Muffliato).

Multicorfors.

Spell list of "N"

Nox (Wand-Extinguishing Charm).

Nebulus.

Spell list of "O"

Oculus Reparo.

Obliteration Charm

Obliviate (Memory Charm).

Obscuro.

Oppugno (Oppugno Jinx).

Orbis

Orchideous

Spell list of "P"

Pack

Patented Musing Charm

Partis Temporus

Periculum

Permanent Sticking Appeal

Peskipiksi Pesternomi.

Petrificus Totalus (Complete Body-Bind Curse).

Piertotum Locomotor.

Placement Appeal

Point Me (Four-Point Spell).

Portus.

Prior Incantato.

Protean Charm

Protego (Guard Appeal).

Protego Diabolica.

Protego Horribilis.

Protego Maxima.

Protego totalum.

Purple Firecrackers

Pus-squirting hex

Spell list of "Q"

Quietus (Quietening Appeal).

Spell list of "R"

Redactum Skullus.

Reducio (Shrinking Appeal).

Reducto (Reductor Curse).

Filling Up Charm

Reparifors

Relashio (Revulsion Jinx).

Rennervate.

Reparifarge.

Reparo (Mending Charm).

Repello Muggletum (Muggle-Repelling Charm).

Repello Inimicum.

Revelio.

Rictusempra (Tickling Charm).

Riddikulus.

Rose Development

Rowboat spell

Spell list of "S"

Salvio Hexia.

Sardine hex.

Scorching Spell.

Scourgify (Combing Appeal).

Sectumsempra.

Shield penetration spell.

Shooting Spell.

Smashing spell.

Serpensortia (Serpent Summons Spell).

Silencio (Silencing Appeal).

Skurge.

Slugulus Eructo (Slug-vomiting Appeal).

Sonorous Charm

Sonorus (Magnifying Charm).

Specialis Revelio (Scarpin's Revelaspell).

Spongify (Softening Charm).

Stealth Sensoring Spell

Steleus.

Stinging Hex, Painful Jinx

Stupefy (Spectacular Spell).

Supersensory Charm

Switching Spell

Spell list of "T"

Taboo

Tarantallegra (Dancing Feet Spell).

Teleportation Spell.

Tentaclifors.

Tergeo.

Titillando (Tickling Hex).

Toenail Development Hex

Tooth-growing spell

Transmogrifian Torture

Trip Jinx

Spell list of "U"

Unbreakable Charm

Unbreakable vow

Undetectable Expansion Charm

Spell list of "V"

Ventus (Ventus Jinx).

Ventus Duo.

Vera Verto.

Verdillious.

Verdimillious.

Verdimillious Duo.

Vipera Evanesca.

Vulnera Sanentur.

Spell list of "W"

Waddiwasi.

Washing up spell

Wingardium Leviosa (Levitation Appeal).

Printed in Poland
by Amazon Fulfillment
Poland Sp. z o.o., Wrocław

64438794R00067